WORDS *of* HOPE *and* HEALING

COMPLICATED GRIEF

How to Understand, Express, *and* Reconcile Your Especially Difficult Grief

Alan D. Wolfelt, Ph.D.

Companion
PRESS

An imprint of the Center for Loss and Life Transition | Fort Collins, Colorado

Companion Press is an imprint of the Center for Loss and Life Transition, 3735 Broken Bow Road, Fort Collins, Colorado 80526.

27   26   25   24   23   22   6   5   4   3   2   1

ISBN: 978-1-61722-318-1

CONTENTS

WELCOME

*"You will lose someone you can't live without, and your heart
will be badly broken, and the bad news is that you never
completely get over the loss of your beloved. But this is also the good
news. They live forever in your broken heart that doesn't seal back
up. And you come through. It's like having a broken leg that never
heals perfectly—that still hurts when the weather gets cold,
but you learn to dance with the limp."*

— Anne Lamott

Coping with a major loss in your life is always difficult, but
sometimes it's *extra* difficult. Have you been experiencing this?
If you're having an especially hard time integrating a death or
other significant loss into your life, my hope is that this little
book will be of help to you.

My goal is to help you understand your extra-challenging grief
and eventually reconcile it into your life. Rest assured that
even if your grief feels extraordinarily painful or complicated,
and even if others have a hard time understanding its intensity,
it is normal. You are normal. Yet at the same time, you are
also deserving of extra-compassionate understanding and

support. In fact, the more overwhelming your grief, the more understanding and support you deserve and will need.

Know that no matter how hurtful, extreme, or challenging your grief may feel right now, you can work your way through it. No, it will not be easy. And no, you will never "get over" the loss. But with time and ongoing, intentional effort—plus, and this is also key in complicated grief, the help of others—you can heal your grieving heart. As Anne Lamott said on the previous page, you can learn to dance with the limp.

If you're a mental-health professional, I invite you also to read my book for caregivers on this topic: *When Grief Is Complicated: A Model for Therapists to Understand, Identify, and Companion Grievers Lost in the Wilderness of Complicated Grief.* It contains much more extensive discussions of the origins of complicated grief as well as the symptoms and categories. In addition, it orients caregivers to the companioning model of complicated grief care and offers numerous suggestions for facilitating active mourning.

I've been a grief counselor, author, and educator for more than four decades now, and throughout those years I have been privileged to bear witness to and support the journey through unfathomable loss and complicated grief many times. These brave grieving people taught me the invaluable lessons I have the honor of sharing with you now. My hope is that you find this resource to be beneficial to you personally and in any efforts you make to help your fellow human beings.

GRIEF AND MOURNING

Grief is anything and everything we think and feel inside after a loss.

We naturally grieve when someone we love dies. But we also grieve when we divorce, experience a health challenge, or separate from a job we are attached to, among many other common life losses, large and small.

And since loss is a normal and unavoidable part of life, our natural human response to loss is also normal. Grief is natural and necessary.

Here's another way of thinking about it: Grief is love's conjoined twin. Grief is what we feel when we are separated from what and who we love. Without love there would be no grief.

So, what is mourning? Mourning is the outward expression of our grief. It's our shared social response to loss. It's our grief gone public. Whenever we cry about a loss, we're mourning. Whenever we talk about it or in any way express our anger, sadness, shock or any other grief thought or feeling about the loss, we're mourning.

Mourning, too, is normal. After all, we're born crying! And as we move through childhood, we continue to cry and wail and protest whenever something we care about is taken away from us. In other words, we mourn. And mourning, like grief, is necessary. Why? Because mourning is how we give momentum to our grief. It's the action that helps us reconcile our grief and integrate it into our life.

COMPLICATED GRIEF AND MOURNING

First, let me say that I believe that *all* grief is complicated to some degree. Just as love is always complex and multifaceted, so too is grief. Whenever someone we love dies, we naturally have lots of different and ever-changing thoughts and feelings about the death. Grief is often profoundly challenging and chaotic. In fact, it's common for grievers to feel like they're going "crazy" because not only is their inner response to the loss so different from their everyday thoughts and feelings, it's disorienting and confusing.

The experience I'm calling "complicated grief" in this book is simply normal grief that's gotten *extra* complicated somehow. It's a matter of the severity of your symptoms, the degree to which they're making it really hard (if not impossible) for you to cope and function day to day, and sometimes the duration of symptoms. These topics will be explored more in the coming pages.

Essentially, complicated grief is normal, necessary grief that has gotten stuck or off track somehow. It has encountered barriers or detours of one kind or another, and as a result has become stalled, waylaid, intensified, or denied altogether. It is *not* abnormal. Instead, it is a normal response in what is almost always an abnormally challenging loss situation.

DIAGNOSTIC TERMINOLOGY

The diagnosis "prolonged grief disorder" was added to the most recent edition, Volume 5, of the American Psychiatric Association's *The Diagnostic and Statistical Manual of Mental Disorders (DSM-5)*. This is the handbook used by psychiatrists, social workers, therapists, and mental-health professionals to assess patients who are struggling with mental-health issues of all kinds.

One year or more after a death, grievers presenting with intense symptoms—such as continual yearning for the person who died, strong emotional pain or numbness, and difficulty moving on with life—may, at the professional's discretion, be given the diagnosis "prolonged grief disorder." To many caregivers, "complicated grief" and "prolonged grief disorder" are synonymous.

I disagree with this diagnosis and the term "disorder" because they pathologize the normal human response to an abnormally difficult loss. Yet I also thought it important to tell you about the diagnostic terminology in case you hear it from your therapist or someone else. In some situations, the diagnosis may even be necessary for your insurance to cover your therapy. What's more, your complicated grief may overlap with clinical depression and/or anxiety disorder. No matter what, I want you to remember that grief and mourning are healthy, normal responses to loss.

To learn more about my thoughts on Prolonged Grief Disorder, see my position paper titled "Grief Is Not a Disorder" at centerforloss.com.

Since grief is the internal response to loss and mourning is the external expression of grief, it's possible you are experiencing complicated mourning as well. What does that mean? It means behaviors that are stuck, intensified, or off track. For example, substance use disorders in the aftermath of a loss are a type of complicated mourning. Self-harming would be another. Aggression, compulsive activities, and depressed behaviors that are visible to others are other examples.

HOW TO USE THIS BOOK

I want you to think of this book as an introduction to understanding your complicated grief. I hope that it will help you get unstuck and embark on a path to hope and healing.

Please understand that this book all by itself is not enough. In my extensive counseling experience, I have learned that people faced with complicated loss, grief, and mourning often benefit from extra support from others. This help can come in many forms (which again, I'll talk more about soon), but chief among them is grief therapy. If you're not already working with a therapist, I hope you will use this book as a steppingstone to getting the extra support you need and deserve.

MY COMPLICATED GRIEF

Please take a minute to jot down a few notes about your understanding of your complicated grief journey so far.

I think my grief is complicated because _____

_____

_____

The following aspects of the loss have been especially hard for me to integrate into my life: _____

_____

_____

These are the thoughts, feelings, and behaviors I've been experiencing lately that make me think my grief is complicated:

_____

_____

_____

I'm reading this book with the hope that _____

_____

_____

THE ORIGINS AND RISK FACTORS OF COMPLICATED GRIEF

"Life is unfair. And it's not fair that life is unfair."
— Edward Abbey

Complicated grief doesn't come out of nowhere. It almost always happens for reasons we can discern and understand. As you're reading, I encourage you to make checkmarks and notes next to anything that might apply to you.

• *Circumstances of the death or loss*
Some types of losses are simply harder to acknowledge and cope with than others. Sudden, unexpected loss is one. Accidental deaths fall into this category, as do military deaths, homicides, suicides, and deaths by sudden illness. In such cases, it's common to feel heightened and ongoing numbness and a sense of unreality. It's also normal for your thoughts to keep returning to the circumstances surrounding the death.

Premature death also applies here. The death of a young person is naturally challenging to acknowledge or understand. Even if the person who died is middle-aged, if their death feels out-of-order—for example, an adult child dying before their parents die—it's as if a rule of nature has been broken.

Cause of death is another big factor. Deaths by suicide, homicide, senseless accidents, military involvement, terrorism, natural disasters, and accidental drug overdose feel especially incomprehensible. In general, the more violent and extreme the circumstances of the death, the more difficult it is for grievers to move beyond shock and numbness, acknowledge the reality of the death, and embrace the pain of the loss—all essential needs in the grieving process.

Long-term illness leading to death can also give rise to complicated grief. Family caregivers to chronically or terminally ill people, for example, start grieving long before the death. This is called "anticipatory grief," and it's normal. By the time the death finally occurs, they are often completely worn down. They're not sure how to feel. And they understandably struggle with transitioning from anticipatory grief to mourning their multifaceted loss, which includes, among other things, a huge void that had been long filled by their caregiving responsibilities.

Finally, deaths with ambiguous causes often give rise to

complicated grief. Sometimes the uncertainty is the result of unknown, confusing, or withheld circumstances or details. For example, in situations where a body is not recovered, it can be difficult to believe the death has even taken place. Our minds and hearts are compelled to understand. I often say that we can cope with what we know, but it is extremely challenging to cope with what we don't know.

• *Your unique personality and history*
Are you introverted or extroverted? Are you good at embracing and expressing emotion in healthy ways? How is your mental health generally? What about your physical health? Do you struggle with any addictions? Do you have a history of conflicted or abusive relationships?

These factors and others related to your personality and unique history may contribute to complicating your grief. Who you were as a unique individual before this loss understandably affects your capacity to cope and integrate the loss now. If you struggle with feeling and expressing emotions, if you have mental or physical health challenges, if you have substance use disorder, and/or if your life history includes abusive, ambivalent, or conflicted relationships with others, these elements of your life experience are likely making it more challenging for you to focus and work on your grief in effective ways.

• *Your relationship with the person who died*

People are unique, and so are their relationships. If your relationship with the person who died was particularly close or complex, you are at greater risk of experiencing complicated grief. So, a potential major complicator of grief naturally ties back to your history of the relationship with person who died.

• *Your loss history*

Loss is a normal part of life. As we grow from children into adulthood, we experience a succession of losses, and we learn to accommodate loss and grief into our lives. Each new grief experience is built upon all former grief experiences. Were any of your previous losses or grief journeys complicated in the ways we're reviewing in this section? If so, you are probably at greater risk of complicated grief now because of the carryover effect.

Multiple losses at the same time or in relatively quick succession are another common contributor to complicated grief. This is called "grief overload." You can be grief overloaded from death losses, of course, but also from a combination of different types of loss.

• *Your support system*

Mourning requires the ongoing support of other human beings in the form of empathy, respect, companionship, and gentle encouragement. Your friends and family often form the foundation of this support system, but yours might also include work colleagues, neighbors, and secondary communities such as faith-based groups or people you share activities with. Essentially, anyone you interact with regularly or feel you can reach out to at any time is potentially in your corner. If you lack a good support network or mistakenly believe you don't need others to help you, your grief is more likely to be complicated.

• *All the current stresses in your life*
Part of the reason that grief is always complicated is that life is always complicated. There are a lot of moving parts—health, education, aging, relationships, children, parents, finances, jobs, social connections, spiritual affiliations, and more. Life is a series of changes: anytime we gain something new, we give something else up.

Do you have other major stress factors going on in your life right now besides the loss? If so, it's no wonder if you're having an extra-hard time coping.

• *Other factors*
There are a number of other things that can contribute to complicated grief. For example, challenging family dynamics, spiritual or religious teachings that discourage mourning, cultural messages that prevent mourners from

openly and honestly expressing emotions or getting help from others, and funeral circumstances that did not permit mourners to share their feelings and gather to support one another. I'm sure you will be able to think of additional factors as well.

MY RISK FACTORS

Now that you've read about the common contributors to complicated grief, I invite you to make a few notes about the reasons your unique grief may be extra complicated. It's OK if you're not sure. Just note anything that came up for you as you read through the section on the origins and risk factors of complicated grief.

_____

_____

_____

_____

_____

_____

_____

_____

_____

_____

SYMPTOMS OF COMPLICATED GRIEF

An effective way to determine if you are struggling with complication of your grief is by exploring the symptoms you experience. The following symptoms are typical in both normal grief and complicated grief. How do you tell the difference? As I mentioned earlier, it's a matter of the severity of your symptoms and the degree to which they're making it difficult (if not impossible) for you to cope and function day to day.

• *Shock, numbness, denial, and disbelief*
These feelings are almost always present in early grief, no matter the circumstances of the death or type of loss. But in complicated grief, these symptoms often persist beyond the early days and weeks and stretch into months and even years. If you feel like you're "stuck" in shock and denial—or that you can't truly believe or acknowledge what happened—you might be experiencing a type of complicated grief I call "unembarked grief" (see page 21).

• *Disorganization, confusion, searching, and yearning*
It's normal for grieving people to feel distracted and
befuddled. It's hard to focus, concentrate, or think straight.
It's also normal to search crowds for the person who died,
expect them to walk through the door at any moment, and
yearn for them to come back to you. If these symptoms are
particularly disruptive and strong for you, however, or if they
have been going on for a long time without slowly easing up,
you may be experiencing complicated grief.

• *Anxiety, panic, and fear*
Another normal feeling after a major loss is anxiety.
Questions naturally demand the attention of our minds and
hearts. *What happens after death? Will I be OK? When and how
will I die? What about others I love? How will I go on without the
person who died?* More practical worries arise, too. *Who will
clean out the person's room or house? What should be done with
their belongings? Is there enough money to keep paying the bills?*

But sometimes the natural stress of grief becomes debilitating
anxiety. When normal concerns turn into anxieties that make
it difficult (if not impossible) for you to function most days,
or if your anxiety has evolved into panic attacks, these are
potential signs that the typical fears of grief have probably
moved into complicated grief territory.

Complicated Grief

• *Explosive emotions*

Anger, rage, hate, blame, resentment, deep frustration, bitterness, and envy/jealousy are emotions that are commonly experienced in grief. I call them collectively the "explosive emotions" because they tend to explode outside of you—sometimes in ways that are harmful to you or others. But they don't always explode—sometimes they fester inside. If you've been harboring explosive emotions without sharing them in some way, they will keep trying to get your attention until you give them the attention they deserve.

The explosive emotions are normal in grief. They are not bad or wrong. They are fundamentally forms of protest. They say, "No! I don't want this to be happening!" They are active emotions that tend to feel better than the more passive, painful feelings of helplessness, sadness, and fear that lie beneath them. In fact, the explosive emotions can protect you from these other feelings, and for a while, that's appropriate, even necessary.

But when explosive emotions turn destructive, and when they don't lessen over time, they are symptoms of complicated grief. Self-harm or self-sabotage, extreme risk-taking, harm to property, and harm to others all cross the line. This includes harm of any kind to yourself or others, including physical, emotional, social, financial, and more.

• *Guilt, regret, and shame*

Guilt and regret are natural feelings after the death of someone loved. Normal grief includes "if-onlys": If only I had told him… If only I had brought her to a different doctor… If only I hadn't… Often such feelings are not logical, but they may be tormenting you nonetheless. Why? Because grief is anchored in love, not logic.

In complicated grief, though, guilt and regret may dominate, and they may not soften over time. In fact, they may act as quicksand in which you can get stuck. Shame, especially, can trap you. Sometimes called the toxic cousin of guilt, shame is a feeling of worthlessness. It tends to be more deep-seated, long-term self-judgment. If you feel like something is inherently wrong with or inadequate about you, that's shame. If your feelings of guilt and regret are pronounced, or if you're routinely experiencing shame as part of your grief, these are potential symptoms of complicated grief.

• *Sadness and depression*

Sadness and depression are natural, authentic emotions after a loss. It's normal for grievers to feel deep pain and a muting of desire and pleasure. While these feelings are naturally difficult to experience, they play an essential role. They force us to regroup—physically, cognitively, emotionally, socially, and spiritually. When we are sad, we instinctively

Complicated Grief

turn inward. We withdraw. We slow down. We need this contemplative, soul-searching time to acknowledge our loss, embrace the pain, sift through memories, think about who we are now, and consider the meaning of it all.

In normal grief, it often takes grievers weeks and months to arrive at the full depth of their sorrow. The pain almost always gets worse before it gets better. But as with the other symptoms explored in this section, when sadness and depression become too debilitating for too long, that often indicates complicated grief. If you're months into your grief journey and still can't function day-to-day or meet your essential obligations because of your depression, you would probably benefit from seeking extra support.

If you're suffering from pronounced sadness or depression, it's important to understand that clinical depression and complicated grief can look and feel a lot alike. If months after the loss you still feel depressed most of the time, find little pleasure in most activities, can't sleep or are sleeping too much, have no energy, feel worthless, can't think or concentrate, have experienced significant weight loss or gain, or have recurring thoughts of your own death or suicide, your complicated grief may now be overlapping with clinical depression. Please make an appointment right away with your primary care provider to discuss therapy and, possibly, antidepressant medication. You may need help rebalancing your biochemistry as a first step on the path to healthy mourning and healing.

CATEGORIES OF COMPLICATED GRIEF

So far we've explored the common reasons why some people develop complicated grief after a loss as well as the common symptoms of complicated grief versus normal grief. In an effort to help you better notice and understand your own potential grief challenges, I'd like to outline the framework I make use of and the main categories of complicated grief.

I often refer to grief as a journey through the wilderness, and my complicated grief category names are drawn from this metaphor.

1. Unembarked grief

Unembarked grief is grief that has never really started. It has never been allowed to depart from the trailhead and enter the normal and necessary wilderness of grief. Some therapists call this "absent," "delayed," or "inhibited" grief. If the loss was months or years ago and you are still feeling mostly numb and in shock over it, you may be experiencing unembarked grief. A lack of pain, sadness, or the other feelings reviewed on pages 15 to 20 is a symptom of unembarked grief. What's more, sometimes life circumstances cause unembarked grief by necessarily delaying or postponing it. If you've had to deal with other urgent matters in your life, such as illness or financial crises, you may have had to set aside the demands of your grief for a while—and now it's time for you to embark. Knowingly or unknowingly, some people also choose to postpone their grief by engaging in long-term denial or avoidance patterns (see Off-trail grief, below).

2. Impasse grief

Imagine you're hiking through the wilderness, and on the trail, you come up against a sheer rock face or a massive downed tree. When you encounter such an obstruction, in order to proceed you must find a way through or around it. In impasse grief, mourners come upon an obstruction and get stuck there. Not only can they not seem to get past the obstruction, they may not even recognize it is an obstruction.

In my grief counseling experience, I have most often seen obstructions in the form of pronounced and prolonged anger, anxiety that has evolved into a tendency to retreat from the world and/or panic attacks, sadness that has become clinical depression, or guilt/shame so all-consuming that the mourner, consciously or unconsciously, is punishing

Complicated Grief

themselves or neglecting to take care of themselves. If you feel stuck on any of these symptoms, especially if they are particularly strong and have not eased over time, you may be experiencing the type of complicated grief I call impasse grief.

3. Off-trail grief

Sometimes people who are grieving take an unhelpful path. It's understandable! After all, it's not like there's a sign in the wilderness of grief with two arrows, one saying, "Healthy grief this way" and the other "Caution! Wrong way!"

The wrong-way grief is usually the path of avoidance. It involves habits and behaviors that the grieving person turns to, often unknowingly, in a subconscious effort to avoid the normal and necessary work of grief and mourning.

Here are some common off-trail patterns:

DISPLACING

Sometimes people in grief take their feelings about a major loss and project them onto another issue or person. If you've been focused on perceived troubles with other people in your life or at work, for example, you might be displacing your normal and necessary grief. The same may be true if you're feeling especially bitter or unhappy about yourself.

REPLACING

After someone very close to them dies, grieving people sometimes quickly move to replace the relationship. Instead of focusing on the painful but necessary work of mourning what was lost, they move to immediately replace it. Forming new relationships can eventually be healthy, but only after a period of mourning and reconciliation. This isn't because of arbitrary social norms requiring a certain number of months or years to grieve but instead because it does take energy and time to psychologically and spiritually integrate such a loss. If you realize you may have prematurely replaced your lost relationship, know that you can still work on acknowledging and mourning your grief.

SOMATICIZING

Physical aches and pains are normal in grief; it's common to not feel well. But if you've been wholly preoccupied with your physical symptoms because they're so severe or distracting, you likely have no energy left to devote to your grief and mourning. "Somaticizing" means converting emotional distress into physical symptoms. It's possible that you're focusing on bodily problems, or perceived physical symptoms, in an unconscious effort to avoid emotional and spiritual pain. I've seen it happen in my grief counseling work many times.

COMPULSIONS/ADDICTIONS

Addictive behaviors such as overworking, overeating, overshopping, and overusing substances are common in grief because they distract us. They feel good in the moment, and they help take the mind and the heart off of the loss. Other compulsions may include gambling, sex, video games, porn, inappropriate risk-taking, over-exercising, and more.

CRUSADING

Crusading grievers convert their grief into over-dedication to, or premature involvement with, a cause. Often the cause is related to the circumstances of the death or the passions of the person who died. Other times grieving people throw themselves into volunteering or leading a grief support group. In the longer run, supporting a cause is an excellent way to discover renewed meaning in life. But in the shorter run, integrating grief first demands acknowledging the loss, befriending the pain, and searching for continued meaning in your life. Skipping ahead to crusading, to the exclusion of mourning, is therefore a potential form of off-trail complicated grief.

4. *Encamped grief*

Sometimes on the journey through grief, people stop moving—forward, backward, or sideways—and instead step off the trail and set up permanent residence. They entrench themselves in their loss experience and sometimes even make it the defining feature of who they are. The hallmark of encamped grief is unending, unchanging distress or fixation with the loss, usually but not always coupled with depression. People experiencing encamped grief are typically preoccupied with the person who died, choosing this obsession over nurturing relationships with family members and friends who are alive. For example, they may keep entire rooms in their home—those associated with the person who died—just as they were for years or decades. While it's good to display photos and hold onto linking objects (special belongings that physically connect mourners to the person who died), long-term shrines such as untouched rooms deny the death and can be a sign of encamped grief. Other clues include spending most of your free time and energy focused on the death and loss. It's even possible to become addicted to the stress of loss because once it is habituated to certain biochemicals, your brain needs regular, ongoing doses of them to feel satisfied.

INVENTORYING YOUR COMPLICATED GRIEF

Now that you've done some more reading and thinking about the possible contributors to, symptoms of, and categories of complicated grief, I'd like you to once again take a look at your own complicated grief experience.

Possible origins of my complicated grief (pp. 9 to 14) include:

_____

_____

_____

My complicated grief symptoms (pp. 15 to 20) have been or
are: _____

_____

_____

Does my complicated grief fit one of the four main categories
(pp. 21 to 26)? If yes or maybe, here's how: _____

_____

_____

_____

Now let's also take a look at your strengths and assets as a
person and a griever. These are the tools you can turn to and
rely on as you actively pursue mourning and healing your
complicated grief.

My positive or helpful current life circumstances: _____

_____

_____

_____

My strong, reliable current relationships: _____

_____

_____

_____

Good memories that sustain me: _____

_____

_____

My personality strengths: _____

_____

_____

_____

My faith or spirituality strengths: _____

_____

_____

_____

My life accomplishments that help me feel capable and/or
secure:_____

_____

_____

MOURNING YOUR COMPLICATED GRIEF

*"When you do nothing, you feel overwhelmed and powerless.
But when you get involved, you feel the sense of hope
and accomplishment that comes from knowing you
are working to make things better."*
— Pauline R. Kezer

How do you integrate complicated grief into your life?
The same way you do all grief: by mourning it openly and
actively, bit by bit, day by day. In other words, mourning
a significant loss is a daily encounter. It's also a daily
commitment.

I understand that it can seem easier or less painful to keep
your grief inside you. If you stay really busy or distracted
with off-trail activities, maybe you can even ignore or
suppress it for long stretches of time. But ultimately,
acknowledging and experiencing your pain inside of you
while also sharing it outside of yourself is necessary for you
to reconcile it. In other words, mourning is work. It takes
time, energy, and attention.

How do you mourn? By giving the necessary attention to the six needs of mourning.

THE SIX NEEDS OF MOURNING

1. **Acknowledge the reality of the death**
    Gently confront the reality that someone you care about has died and will never physically be present in your life again.

2. **Embrace the pain of the loss**
    Recognize that the pain of grief is normal and necessary, and allow yourself to feel it fully when it arises.

3. **Remember the person who died**
    Spend time recalling memories and sharing them with others.

4. **Develop a new self-identity**
    Consider anew who you are now and what you want for yourself moving forward.

5. **Search for meaning**
    Question the meaning and purpose of life, and discover meaning for your life moving forward.

6. **Let others help you—now and always**
    Maintain and build relationships with others, both for grief support and for connection and companionship moving forward.

As you work your way through the steps ahead, you will be making good use of the six needs of mourning. Know that every time you honestly and actively engage with one or more of the six needs of mourning, you will be creating divine momentum to eventually reconcile your grief into your life.

THE FIVE STEPS OF INTEGRATING COMPLICATED GRIEF

Step 1: Set your intention

Recognizing that you must first set your intention is critical to ultimately being able to integrate your grief into your life. Without this consciousness about doing what you need to do, there is risk that you will continue to feel like you are simply drowning in your grief with little or no movement.

What do you hope to achieve by better understanding and mourning your loss? Where would you like to be physically, emotionally, cognitively, socially, and spiritually a year from now? What are your goals for your grief work? What do you most hope for the future for yourself and those closest to you?

Write down your intention(s) here: _____

_____

_____

_____

_____

_____

Step 2: Acknowledge the challenge

This grief you are struggling with now is probably different than other griefs you have experienced in your life. It's more painful. It's more obtrusive into your thoughts and feelings. It's more disruptive of your life. It's making it more difficult for you to go on.

All of this is normal given the origins and risk factors we talked about on pages 9 to 14. Rest assured that you have been doing the very best you knew how to do with your extra-complicated grief and loss circumstances.

Now, having set your intention and acknowledged the challenges that are ahead of you, you are ready to commit yourself to coming out of the dark and into the light.

Step 3: Honor and overcome resistance

How did you feel when you read through Step 2? Did you feel yourself resist the idea that you will need to commit yourself to the hard work of mourning to understand and integrate your complicated grief? If so, know that this resistance, too, is normal.

Some people experiencing complicated grief fear that if they start really focusing on and expressing their deepest thoughts and feelings, they'll never be able to stop. Others are afraid of revealing to someone else what they feel inside or admitting to behaviors they feel ashamed of because they worry they're "not normal" or are "going crazy." And some are reluctant to befriend the pain of the loss because they see it as not serving a purpose or they lack an understanding of the role of hurt in healing. They might question, "Why would I choose to embrace pain? It won't bring back the person that I lost who I valued."

Rest assured that any resistance you feel is normal. Notice the resistance, thank it for trying to protect you, and then work to find ways to overcome it. My hope is that the following steps will give you the courage needed to help you work with the natural resistance you may be feeling.

Step 4: Reach out for help

Identifying and reaching out to compassionate helpers is always essential in grief. It's the sixth need of mourning (p. 30), and it's even more essential in complicated grief. Grief is a solo activity because it happens inside you. But I remind you that by definition mourning is "the shared response to loss." We all need and deserve to get help when we have sorrows of the soul.

I hope you have friends and family members who listen with kindness and compassion whenever you want to talk about your grief. Even when you aren't talking about your loss, simply having them nearby can help you feel loved and supported. If you don't have a good social support network, on the other hand, or if you aren't opening up to your friends and family, you will be well-served to seek outside support.

But even if you do have a good support network and routinely talk to them about your loss, I still encourage you to find a grief-informed counselor/therapist. As you may have come to realize, complicated grief is usually too challenging to integrate all on your own. As previously noted, it is often the result of a complex (and often longstanding) interplay of loss circumstances and risk factors. What's more, your friends and family only have so much time and empathy to give. Your mourning needs may well be too intense and frequent for them to support. Adding a good, trained grief counselor/therapist to your support team has the potential of being a tremendous help to you.

Grief counselors can range from therapists to clergy, hospice caregivers, funeral home aftercare staff, and lay-trained caregivers. Grief therapists, on the other hand, usually have specific interest, training, and experience in helping people with complications of their grief.

As someone experiencing complicated grief, you have special needs, and so you need specialized care. As you consider potential grief counselors/therapists, you will want to attempt to find someone who does not simply provide grief support but specializes in complicated or traumatic grief. Call your local hospice to see if they have a recommendation, or ask your primary-care provider. A local information and referral service, such as a crisis intervention center, might maintain a list of grief therapists in your area, as might your local hospital, family service agency, funeral homes, and/or mental-health clinic.

If there are several, consider scheduling an initial consultation with each of them so you can see who might be the best fit for you. After you choose, you may find that it will take you a few sessions to decide if you and your therapist are a good match for your needs. If it's not a good match, continue to search for the right therapist for your unique needs.

In my experience, some people with complicated grief need only a few sessions with a grief-informed therapist, while others benefit from a longer-term therapeutic relationship. In general, I find that it's best for people with complicated grief to commit themselves to working with a therapist for as long as it takes to integrate their grief. With complicated grief, it can take time to uncover all the contributing factors, understand the six needs, and then find ways to actively and effectively mourn.

Grief therapy works because it provides a supportive

environment and structure in which you are encouraged to actively encounter and express your grief. It's your therapist's job to help facilitate your active mourning, offer you empathetic listening and encouragement, and affirm that you are doing the work needed, even when it's painful. Because I remind you, the only way to the other side is through.

Depending on the size of your community, it may be challenging to find a qualified local therapist to work with your complicated grief. Therefore, keep in mind the possibility of reaching out for help online. The good news is, today there are many online therapists who may be of help to you. Another source of potential referral is the Association for Death Education and Counseling (adec.org), which can assist you in finding specialized grief therapists for your needs.

A caution: Regardless of the length of your therapy, it's doubtful you'll always feel you are steadily moving forward in your grief journey. More likely, the natural ebb and flow of pain and healing will at times make you feel you aren't making progress or are even going backward. This is normal. Be patient with yourself as you continue to work on the six needs of mourning, and trust the process. As long as you are actively mourning, you are doing the work you need to do.

Complicated Grief

SHOULD YOU ALSO JOIN A GRIEF SUPPORT GROUP?

Participating in a good grief support group is a wonderfully healing mourning activity for many grievers. For some people, there's nothing more affirming than openly sharing thoughts and feelings among compassionate, nonjudgmental, and understanding fellow journeyers.

However, complicated grief is often too complicated or unique for a typical support group to respond to. So, before you join any support group, in person or online, I suggest talking it over with your therapist about whether it's a good fit for your current needs.

Step 5: *Actively allow yourself to mourn*
Mourning is anything that involves expressing your grief outside of yourself in some way. It's giving attention to your grief via active, intentional engagement with your thoughts and feelings.

Common mourning activities include:

- Crying, sobbing, wailing, yelling
- Talking to a friend, family member, or mentor about your loss
- Writing in a journal (private but still external expression)
- Writing to others—online, via email, or on paper
- Sharing online, such as on social media or a grief forum

- Participating in a support group
- Making art that expresses your feelings
- Doing any activity with others during which you also talk about the loss at least a bit
- Praying about or meditating on your loss
- Moving your body, preferably in nature, while talking aloud—to yourself or to the person who died—about your grief
- Carrying out a mourning ritual of some kind, such as candle-lighting

As you do the work of mourning, you'll probably discover other mourning activities that work well for you.

DOSING YOUR MOURNING

As I've said, mourning is a daily (or nearly daily) activity. It's not something that can be done and completed in a brief period of time. You can't heal grief—especially complicated grief—in an intensive few days or weeks. Instead, mourning will soften your complicated grief over the course of months and sometimes years, but only if it's done in small, regular *doses*.

The good news about dosing your mourning is that you don't have to actively and intentionally express your grief for hours each day to begin to feel like you're making headway.

In fact, I would advise against spending too much focused time on your grief each day. Yes, your grief will still be there in the background every day, perhaps all day, and you may still have entire days where you will feel generally depressed or anxious. I am not saying you won't grieve every day. What I am saying is that you should dose your *active* mourning one day at a time, spending maybe fifteen minutes up to an hour on an intentional mourning activity and then turning to other activities that give you physical, cognitive, emotional, social and spiritual respite until the next day.

If you establish this dosing routine, you will find that after a few weeks your background grief may start to ease up a little. That's because you will be giving it focused, productive daily doses of attention. You will be acknowledging and honoring it. You will be creating an outlet through which it can flow, thus relieving some of the internal pressure. You will be giving it momentum toward reconciliation.

TRYING YOUR THERAPIST'S SUGGESTIONS

In addition to taking advantage of mourning opportunities that naturally arise for you, as well as intentionally planning others into your daily routines, you will probably want to try various mourning techniques that your therapist suggests. After all, your therapist is noticing where you need to give particular attention to the six needs of mourning, and will probably invite you to engage in activities that will allow you to focus on them.

For example, if your complicated grief understandably focuses on the cause of the death, your therapist may suggest that you visit the location the death took place— perhaps accompanied by them. This is called exposure therapy, and it's been shown to help grieving people more deeply acknowledge the reality of a death and make the scary unknown known and thus less frightening. Exposure therapy isn't always appropriate, of course, but it's the kind of technique that can really make a difference for some mourners in some circumstances.

Another example is memory work. The third need of mourning is to remember the person who died, but sometimes mourners are reluctant to spend time and energy remembering because it's too painful. If your therapist asks you to bring in photos, write down stories, or share memories associated with the loss or the person who died, that's because these activities are necessary to help you integrate the loss into your ongoing life. In grief, we often have to go backward before we can go forward. A big part of grief therapy, in fact, is helping you befriend the complete, unedited version of your story. So yes, remembering can hurt, but in my counseling experience mourners almost always find treasures amidst the pain and also tend to feel a huge sense of relief after exploring memories. They learn that it's OK—even good—to remember. They learn that the pain softens through memory work. And they learn that they are strong, capable people with complex life stories that need to be remembered, honored, and told.

USING A MOURNING MAP

I also invite you to take a look at the Mourning Map on the next page. This is a tool you can fill out with your therapist, not all at once but instead session by session, dose by dose, as opportunities, insights, and divine momentum naturally occur.

Divine momentum, by the way, is the experience of being propelled toward healing by doing what is necessary and helpful in grief. Sometimes after you've actively worked on one or more of the six needs of mourning, you may notice that you feel a bubble of hope or buoyed by a sense of movement toward reconciliation. In other words, you feel a little better and a little more hopeful about the future. This is the power of divine momentum.

MOURNING MAP

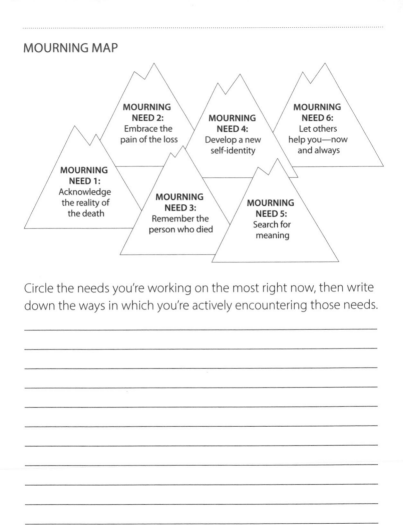

MOURNING NEED 1: Acknowledge the reality of the death

MOURNING NEED 2: Embrace the pain of the loss

MOURNING NEED 3: Remember the person who died

MOURNING NEED 4: Develop a new self-identity

MOURNING NEED 5: Search for meaning

MOURNING NEED 6: Let others help you—now and always

Circle the needs you're working on the most right now, then write down the ways in which you're actively encountering those needs.

_____

_____

_____

_____

_____

_____

_____

_____

_____

_____

_____

_____

_____

Short-term grief goals: _____

_____

_____

_____

_____

_____

_____

Long-term grief goals:_____

_____

_____

_____

_____

_____

_____

_____

What questions or concerns do you have related to encountering
any of these needs? _____

_____

_____

_____

_____

_____

_____

_____

_____

_____

RECONCILING YOUR COMPLICATED GRIEF

Grief never ends, but it can be integrated into your life story. We as human beings don't resolve or recover from our grief but instead become reconciled to it.

Each day that you intentionally and actively mourn your grief, you are taking a step toward reconciliation. The sharp, ever-present pain of your grief will begin to soften, and you will start to experience:

- Stable and ideally healthy eating and sleeping patterns
- Energy and wellbeing
- Healthy relationships
- Enjoyment
- A renewed sense of meaning and purpose

Reconciliation emerges much in the way grass grows. We don't typically check our lawns each day to see if the grass is growing, but it does grow, and soon we come to realize it's time to mow the grass again. Likewise, we can't expect to examine our reconciliation on a daily or weekly basis to be assured that we're healing. Nonetheless, as long as we're consistently doing the work of mourning, we do eventually realize, over the course of months and years, that we've come a long way.

In complicated grief, you may find that the time you spend working with your therapist will give you good momentum toward reconciliation but won't get you all the way there. If so, that's OK. The purpose of therapy is to get you on the right track. You will simply need to continue to intentionally, actively grieve and mourn on your own. I suggest making intermittent follow-up appointments with your therapist after your weekly sessions are complete. Ask your therapist about meeting with them three months later, then six months after that, then a year after that, followed by annual check-ups if the two of you agree it's a good idea.

Just as grief is normal, reconciliation of grief is normal. Complicated grief takes extra time and effort to reconcile, but it is doable and absolutely worth it. In fact, nothing is more worthwhile than living the rest of your precious days here on earth as fully and with as much meaning and purpose as possible.

For additional criteria related to reconciliation of your grief, see my book *Understanding Your Grief: Ten Essential Touchstones for Finding Hope and Healing Your Heart (Second Edition)*.

SELF-CARE
FOR PEOPLE EXPERIENCING
COMPLICATED GRIEF

"Do something today that your future self will thank you for."
— Author Unknown

As you are actively, intentionally mourning in small doses each day, it's also nonnegotiable that you simultaneously focus on your self-care. You might be reflecting: *How am I supposed to exercise, eat right, etc. when I barely have enough energy and focus to get out of bed, go grocery shopping, or do laundry?* It's a fair question.

The answer is that self-care in grief is about attitude as much or more than it is about a to-do list. If you simply move through your days with the attitude that you need and deserve good care, you are more likely to make small choices that serve you well. When it comes to self-care, it's the little things that are the big things.

PRACTICE SELF-COMPASSION

I hope you will remind yourself each and every day to be self-compassionate. You have experienced misfortune. You are suffering. You need and deserve understanding and tender, loving care—from others and from yourself. You need lots of rest, comfort, and kindness.

There's a fine line between self-pity and self-compassion, though. If you are self-pitying, you are thinking of yourself as a victim. You are emphasizing that you have been wronged and are uniquely burdened. Self-pity tends to say "poor me." If you are practicing self-compassion, on the other hand, you are seeing yourself within the context of humanity. Yes, you may have been wronged, and yes, you are struggling, but you are not alone.

Self-compassion acknowledges that life has its challenges for almost all of us. It brings perspective. It reminds us of our connections to and similarities with many. And it builds empathy for ourselves as well as others.

CULTIVATE PATIENCE

Healing complicated grief is hard work. And it usually takes a long time, even when you are proactively dosing your mourning day after day, week after week.

If and when you're feeling impatient, I'm asking you to trust the process you are now engaged in. You probably won't start feeling better right away. If you feel worse for a while, that's not unusual. As I previously noted, even in normal grief, as you do the work of mourning, the pain typically gets harder before it gets easier.

As long as you're actively mourning and getting reliable support from other people, you're doing what you need to do. If you're a naturally impatient person, you're going to need to intentionally cultivate patience. Meditation and other mindfulness practices can help you with this.

TAKE GOOD CARE OF YOURSELF

You take good care of yourself with small, effective daily habits. It's really that simple. If your current habits aren't helping you feel comforted, rested, healthy, stronger, mindful, and well supported, don't despair. Research shows that incorporating better habits isn't about willpower and big goals—instead, it's about starting really small and building from there.

As you read through the following self-care suggestions, choose one or two things to start doing right now. If they're daily activities, schedule them into your day.

Behavioral scientists who've studied this say that the best way to commit to a new habit is to attach it to an ingrained habit. This is called "habit stacking." For example, if you need to drink more water, get in the habit of pouring yourself a glass of water before you sit down to watch your evening TV. Or if you regularly listen to music, podcasts, or audiobooks, add the habit of putting on your walking shoes before you begin. Take a short walk as you begin listening. If TV watching is more your thing, stack a few minutes of yoga poses, stationary biking, or lifting hand weights on top of your TV time.

Here are the most important fundamentals of self-care:

Physical

First, see a physician. After your initial visit, schedule regular check-ups and screenings so you can ward off any problems before they get serious. Your doctor may also help you with any grief-related sleep and mood problems that may be preventing you from functioning well day-to-day and focusing on healthy mourning.

Next, though the natural lethargy of grief may be dragging you down, your body needs movement to stay healthy. If weeks or months have passed since the loss and you're not getting enough physical activity, just start paying attention to your daily step count and try to increase it. It's OK if you're starting at 1,000 steps a day. The next day, do 1,200. Then try for 1,500. Work your way up to 5,000-10,000 steps a day if you can. You don't need to join a gym or run 5Ks to get physically healthier. And you'll find that doing physical movement you enjoy—especially outdoors—will lift your spirits and help you sleep better.

Finally, be aware of what you put into your body. Food choices and hydration can have a big effect on your mood. Again, you don't have to totally change your diet. Simply try to eat a few more vegetables and fruits and a little less saturated fat and salt each day. Be sure you're drinking enough water, too.

Cognitive
Grief naturally disrupts the mind. As previously discussed, it's normal for grievers to feel distracted, dazed, bewildered, forgetful, and confused. Through active mourning, you will be helping your mind acknowledge and integrate the loss, but during the months or years in which this is happening, your brain also needs accommodation and respite.

If you're not thinking well these days, give your mind a break in any way you can. Let go of optional commitments for   . the time being. Don't take on any tasks or projects that feel overwhelming. Trust your intuition. If you can take some time off work, do so. If you can't, talk to your supervisor about your need for a role that is less taxing. Ask for help with tasks that seem too cognitively stressful to you right now. Examples might be preparing your taxes or sorting the belongings of the person who died. Friends often want to help but don't know how. They may feel relief and gratitude at being asked to assist you with specific practical tasks.

And if you're ruminating too often on your loss—if your mind keeps returning to it over and over and over and you can't seem to get away from thinking about it—try writing your thoughts down for half an hour. Promise your mind you'll return to another writing session tomorrow. This habit can create a loss thinking time and place that satisfies the grieving mind.

Emotional

You are wounded emotionally. What makes you feel emotionally soothed and supported? What relaxes you? What makes you feel calmer and more at ease? These things will be different for each person. Incorporate at least one or two into each and every day.

"Comfort" items and activities help many of us. Things like taking a warm bath, sitting outside in the sun, drinking tea, listening to your favorite music, gazing at the flames in a fireplace, getting a massage, practicing breathing exercises, watching your favorite movie, hugging a loved one, and cuddling with a pet can all have the effect of slowing your heart rate, lowering your blood pressure, relaxing your muscles, and balancing your biochemistry.

Of course, active mourning is also emotional self-care. When you are intentionally encountering and expressing your grief, you are caring for your emotional self. Those moments are often painful and challenging, however, so it's also important to counterbalance them with comforting, restful, and fun activities that have nothing to do with grief.

Social

In grief, social self-care means finding a balance between allowing yourself to appropriately withdraw when you need to and reaching out for connection and hope on a regular basis.

You need others to help you with your grief. When you are actively mourning, you need nonjudgmental listening ears and kindness. And when you aren't actively mourning, you need company. You need to be around other people, and you need to share experiences with other people. All of this is essential to healing in grief and to finding meaning in your ongoing life.

If you're an introvert, you might need to "put yourself out there" more than you normally would. Again, think small. Commit to connecting with at least one other person once a day by texting, emailing, phoning, or catching up face-to-face. It's even better if you are able to do something together in person. Over time, work on adding social activities to your life that feel meaningful to you. Remember that good relationships don't just happen. They require proximity, repetition, and quality time.

I understand, however, that complicated grief can be socially challenging. If the circumstances of your loss are stigmatized in any way and have thus put a strain on your relationships, or if others don't know how to broach the subject with you, you may need to be the one to reach out and put people at ease. Let them know you're struggling with the loss and that it's good to talk about it.

Spiritual

Grief is first and foremost a spiritual journey because it forces us to confront the biggest questions: *Why are we here? What is life for? What happens after death? What is the meaning of all of this?*

Spiritual self-care means making time for your spirit each day. What makes you feel spiritually grounded? What spiritually centers and calms you? What gives you a sensation of awe or a feeling of gratitude? Whatever your answers to these questions may be, add activities that include them to your daily schedule.

For some people, solitary activities such as prayer and/or meditation form the foundation of spiritual self-care. For others, more social spiritual activities are important, such as religious services or group yoga. Do what works for you.

If the loss has caused you to feel disconnected or distant from your spiritual self, or you feel like your divine spark is extinguished, please talk to your therapist about this. An important part of your grief work will be recreating your spiritual identity.

FOSTER HOPE

Hope is an expectation of a good that is yet to be. It's a future-looking knowledge felt in the present moment. In grief, hope is a belief that healing can and will unfold, and that despite the loss and current pain, there will surely be many opportunities for meaning and purpose in the years to come.

Active mourning is the most important way to build hope in complicated grief. This might sound counterintuitive because mourning is also painful, but as you actively and intentionally dose yourself with the six needs of mourning, dose by dose, day by day, you will find that your loss is slowly becoming integrated into your ongoing life. You will be reconciling your complicated grief while also, at the same time, revising your self-identity, finding meaning in moving forward, and strengthening relationships with others.

Yes, you will still and always grieve because you will still and always love the person who died. But your ongoing love and grief will become an integrated, manageable part of today, tomorrow, and all the precious tomorrows you have yet to come.

Ultimately, doing the hard work of reconciling great loss feels satisfying, even meaningful. What else feels meaningful?

Love. Healthy relationships. Self-care. Enjoyment. Meaningful activities and experiences. Besides active mourning, these are the building blocks of hope. Build them into your hours, days, weeks, and months.

A FINAL WORD

"My joy may be diminished now,
but I am still alive to be more joyful ahead."
— Ankam Nithin Kumar

Complicated grief arises from the most difficult experiences and circumstances that human life can, unfortunately, present us with. There is no doubt that you have been torn apart. No wonder you're struggling. No wonder you need extra understanding and support.

Again, I encourage you to get the support you both need and deserve. If you're not already working with a therapist, please consider making some calls today. If you're aware that you don't have the energy or follow-through to make that first appointment, then talk to a friend or family member and ask them to help you take this one step. You don't need to walk alone, and you don't even need to take the first step alone.

Remember, your therapist and the principles in this little book will help you move toward reconciling your grief. I hope you will pick it up whenever your spirits are low or you need an extra boost of affirmation or encouragement.

You have a lot to grieve and mourn, but you also have a lot to look forward to. I say this with certainty because I have companioned many people who have lived through complicated grief and loss.

I hope we meet one day.

ABOUT THE AUTHOR

Alan D. Wolfelt, Ph.D., is a respected author and educator on the topics of companioning others and healing in grief. He serves as Director of the Center for Loss and Life Transition and is on the faculty at the University of Colorado Medical

 School's Department of Family Medicine. Dr. Wolfelt has written many bestselling books on healing in grief, including *Understanding Your Grief, Healing Your Grieving Heart*, and *Grief One Day at a Time*. Visit www.centerforloss.com to learn more about grief and loss and to order Dr. Wolfelt's books.

When Grief is Complicated

After a significant loss, grief is normal and necessary. But sometimes a mourner's grief becomes naturally heightened, stuck, or made more complex by especially difficult circumstances, such as suicide, homicide, or multiple losses within a short time period. This is called "complicated grief."

In this primer by one of the world's most respected grief educators, Dr. Wolfelt helps caregivers understand the various factors that often contribute to complicated grief. He presents a model for identifying complicated grief symptoms and, through real-life examples, offers guidance for companioning mourners through their challenging grief journeys. This book rounds out Dr. Wolfelt's resources on the companioning philosophy of grief care, making it an essential addition to your professional library.

ISBN: 978-1-61722-258-0 · **242 pages** · softcover · $24.95

All Dr. Wolfelt's publications can be ordered by mail from:
Companion Press, 3735 Broken Bow Road, Fort Collins, CO 80526
(970) 226-6050 • www.centerforloss.com